FOR THE BROKEN II

by Shenaia Lucas

this book
is my heart
in your hands

-be kind

continuing the brave story
of healing and loving
despite breaking and dying

-we live on

CHAPTERS

chapter one

for the healing

the process
of healing
does not end
when the wounds
are no longer
visible

-it ends when the wounds no longer
ache

you don't
have to
know
the path ahead
to walk it

*-beginning is the most important
thing*

i never wanted
to learn
to live
without you

-*experience is a cruel teacher*

we are human
but that
does not excuse
our flaws

-no excuse

how
can the future
live

while
the past
breathes
its oxygen?

-the mind often forgets

change the locks
on the door
to your heart

-it's time to heal

you were caught
in his web
of lies

it's time
to break free

-*while you still can*

do not let him
make you
like him

push away his darkness
and emanate light

-resist

blood
gushed out

but

these wounds
will heal

-*the pain of healing*

she packed away
her belongings
in a borrowed
suitcase

she left him
before he awoke
in the morning

-*escapism*

all
the sweet nothings

all
the loving words

all
our time together

-he never told the truth

the heart aches
speaking feelings
the tongue
could never
fathom

-*esoteric*

he told you
you were meant
for each other

but adam and eve
were meant
for happiness

it's all
about
choices

-and the time for yours is now

let him taste
the bitterness
that has rotted
your soul
away

give him
a smile
and watch
his world
crumble

-*sweet revenge*

let's be honest
he's not worth
your time

-you are a goddess

he doesn't know
what he wants

that should tell you
who you don't

-want

exhale
him

-don't forget to breathe

you can
never become
the woman
you were meant
to be

by
wallowing
in the grave
of your misery

adapt
with the times
find
a patch of sun
and grow

-sunlight

he
broke you

but you
are stronger
than his poison

-the antidote

you miss
the sunshine
of joy

but do not
forget

that just
as a flower
needs
sunshine
and
rain

you
need
sadness
too
sometimes

-*sadness can nourish you too*

the caterpillar
hated the view
from the ground

-nothing lasts forever

spring will come
the butterfly
will emerge
from the cocoon

-and you will too

the grave
is not yet
here
for you

so live on
another day

-*what do you have to lose*

ignore him

you are not
too much

you are
exactly
what you
should be

-*a full glass*

let it die
and grow roses
on the grave

-recycling

do not cry
over a man
whose masculinity
is so fragile
that he
would not cry
over you
too

-the minimum

like the falling
of autumn leaves
the season comes
to drop
dead things

-you were out of love a month ago

watch
how he speaks
of his exes

for that
is how he
will speak
about you

*-mature men respect their past
partners*

you will sleep
restfully
again

don't worry
give yourself time
to heal

-heal the mind

chapter two

for the erasing

if you need to change
to keep him

keep changing
but not
for him

throw him out
and change
your taste

-the real problem

if he
does not value
your heart

as you value
his

you cannot
trust him

to protect
the vulnerable places
you show to him

-trust

on the bathroom floor
you find yourself
puking out your guts
pushing away
the thought
of your brokenness

but a broken bottle
cannot make
you whole

-*take back your life in the morning*

you can never
get high enough
to escape
the atomic bomb
of heartbreak

-fallout

you are so compassionate
trying to heal
every broken soul
that comes your way
always giving
and giving

but you cannot give away
what you do not have
yourself

-*wisdom*

one day
the constellations
of your heart
will drift
into place
and everything
will make sense
at last

-*be patient*

cry
into your pillow

release
your inner sadness

-the importance of letting it all out

you were flawless
and whole

i was cracked
and shattered

it was the right person
at the wrong time

-fate can be cruel

you are
the tsunami
wiping away
what resists you

you are the power
of nature
coursing through
your veins

-*victory is certain*

collect
your tears

create
a perfume
from them

let it be
a badge
of honor

-battles won

do not
let him love you
unless
he is prepared
to play
with fire

-you are the flame

sometimes
it is all too much
and you need
to stop
the relentless
revolutions
of the earth
lest
you fall off it

-call in sick today

you are not broken
you are bruised
you are stronger
than you think

-hope in the morning

the greatest struggle
is never knowing why
when the question
hangs there
in mid air
begging
for an answer

sometimes
the mystery
hurts more
than
the pain.

-*closure*

your past
does not haunt you

your past
is the foundation
you will build
upon

-*scars heal*

take heart
and let your soul
be anchored
by your
enduring
hope

-the ocean is merciless

if you learned from it
it wasn't
just
a mistake

-*mistakes*

you are not
the raincloud
following
others
around

you
are a ball
of sunshine
erasing shadows
wherever
they are found

-*you are the light*

pull
the knife
out from
your back

and carve
your initials
into the tree
at the top
of the highest
mountain

-survival

you are not
a tragic story
you are
a hero's journey
in waiting

-potential

he ran his fingers
along my scars
and i shivered
feeling more whole
than i had
before

-beautiful

chapter three

for the loving

i've been chasing
after an idea of love
that only exists
as just that

an idea

-fantasy

day by day
brick by brick
we build
something
beautiful

-castles

love
is effortless
except
when
it isn't

-exceptions

pull back
the curtains

let
the performance
begin

-*actress*

i hope
we are like birds
who leave
for a season
but always
return

-return

kiss me
under a thousand
city lights

or kiss me
in a supermarket
parking lot

i don't care
just kiss me

-*real*

we fell
out of love
like falling
out of a chair

in slow motion
and then instantly

-out

what is it
about a whispered
"i love you"
that sends shivers
down my spine
every time

-*simple*

you have
my heart
for as long
as you want it

-yours

we have both
forgotten
the sunlight

lets find
happiness
in each other

-*together*

never fake

a smile
a promise
an orgasm
or anything
else

give me
something
real

-fake

sleep
with me

-*intimacy*

please, please
just show me
you care

-*effort*

life is too short
to love
with anything less
than everything
you are

-give me everything

burn
the love notes

they were all lies
anyway

-*tragic ends*

we
are
still
young

-don't give up on me

is it so
unbelievable
that this
could last
forever?

-forever

if you love me
break me
in ways
i've never
been broken
before

-new

your name
is my favorite sound
i have ever heard

-*sounds*

love is beautiful
until
it is not

-*everything good ends*

i love the way
you make
everything
seem alright

-*everything*

let us
approach
love
like
a great
craft

devoting
time
discipline
and
effort

-to create something beautiful

the earth may shake
my heart may stop
but i
will love you
beyond death

-ghosts

chapter four

for the oppressed

their culture
is not
a decoration

-do not steal

baby boomers
are the most
fucking entitled
generation
of all time

-baby boomers

caitlyn jenner
is not
a trans
role
model

-no

when you
reach success
its important
to send
the ladder
back down

-upward together

i yearn
to see a woman
in the white house
before i die

-*i'm with her*

remember
that god
will not
leave you
in the depths
of darkness

he will lift you
out of your misery
for he will never
give you
more
than you
can take

-god

you may be
downtrodden
broken
on the edge
of giving up

but do not fear
for you
will break through

-breakthrough

sometimes
all you can do
is plug in
your headphones
and drown out
the noise

-*noise*

why
do they always speak
about minority
representation
in films
and tv shows

as if its some
kind of
burden?

-we are not a burden

fuck
the patriarchy

-patriarchy

the tea party
is the party
of the rich

-liars

women
are not
props

-*x*

if a woman
wants
to have sex
its none
of your
fucking business

stop being
so goddamn concerned
about the sex lives
of other people

-*xxx*

love
is love
is love
is love
is love
is love
is love
is love
is love
is love
is love
is love
is love
is love
is love

-lgbtq

cellulite
is not
ugly

the attitude
of society
that shames
people
for their genetics

is
what's ugly

-ugly

society
is always itching
to point fingers
of
blame
shame
derision
and
hatred
towards women

there's nothing
they hate more
than a woman
who stands up
for herself

-*pointing fingers*

our nation
is far too diverse
to be run
by a country club
of old white men

we are more
than that
and we
could do
so much
better

-*diverse*

our artists
run
on
depression

-i

the moment
a woman
becomes
successful

they crucify
everything they can
about her

-*shame*

we are not
so far removed
from the evil times
we read about
in history books

it wasn't
that long ago
and its effects
are still going on
today

discrimination
is alive and well
and it's our turn
to fight
the good fight
against it

wherever
it rears
its ugly head

-*discrimination*

men
are not
the
default

-default

you
are

alive

-act like it

the way
the world
brushes aside
the young
bright minds
of minorities
is sickening

-the future

it doesn't matter
what you were wearing
what time you were out
the length of your skirt
your tone of voice
or anything else

you were NOT
asking for it

it was NOT
your fault

the blame
rests
with the perpetrator
NOT
with you

-it will never be your fault

we need
to start treating
animals
a whole lot
better

-*fuck seaworld*

this is not
a man's world

this is a world
of equal opportunity

this is a world
where our voices
matter

it's not perfect
yet
but every day
we must fight
to advance
the voices
of women
all around
the world

-all around the world

chapter five

for the broken

if you
are feeling
lonely

don't forget
to seek the company
of yourself
first
and
foremost

-lonely

the same legs
that cause you
to stumble
will allow you
to rise

-*weakness from strength*

it may not be
today
but one day
you will find
so much beauty
from the ashes
of your current situation

you will see
all the light
that was waiting
to burst forth
from this darkness

it may not be
today
but one day
you will
find the strength
to rise
from the ashes

and be reborn
into something
so much more
beautiful

than you
could ever
have imagined

-beauty from pain

the most
broken
of people
carry
the most beautiful
secrets

never
take it
for granted

if they
open up
to you

-*open up*

never forget
that all the time
you spend
thinking
about the past

chips away
at the present moment

let the past
die

let the present
breathe

-*let the present breathe*

you
are not
a burden

you
are not
hard to love

you
are not
a liability

you
are beautiful

you
are joy

you
are strong

and you
are not defined
by what they say

-defined

only a weak man
is afraid
of a powerful woman

do not
censor yourself

do not
dumb yourself down

do not
change

for any man

you are perfect
as you are

-*as you are*

human beings
are so
beautiful

in the way
they turn
pain
and suffering

into beauty
and love

-*transmutation*

if he
would not
cross an ocean
for you

or fight
a dragon

if he
would not
do the most
for you

why
should you
do anything
for him?

-would he?

you deserve
to be treated
like the
queen
(or king)
you are

-*you are royalty*

it will be
difficult
it will be
a tough road

but you
are nothing
if not
strong enough

for you
can do
so much more
than you think
you can

-*more*

love
feels like

sacrifice
forgiveness
patience
kindness

before it
feels
like
butterflies

if it's never tough
if its never work
if its never a struggle

that's not love
that's fiction

embrace reality
and love people
with all their rough edges
all their imperfections

love them
the way
real people
need to be loved

-real love

sometimes
the most important thing
is just
to keep
moving

keep trudging on
keep pushing forward

even when it feels
like you're marching
through wet cement
on the road
to hell

remember
to move

because
an inch
of progress
if that's all you've got today
is still
progress

-keep moving

turn your eyes
upward
to freedom

-upward

it's not
over
yet

your story
has just
begun

the morning
has not yet
dawned

so lift your head
it's not over

and you've
still got
a fight
left
in you

-*fight*

i know
your heart
has shattered
again

i know
your dreams
have fallen
apart

i know
your world
is like dust
in the wind

but remember
that this isn't the end

you
will
rise

to face the day

-*rise*

never forget
that your simplest actions
can have
the biggest consequences

never forget
that a smile
to a homeless man
may stop him
from ending it all
and you
can save a life
with a gentle touch

never forget
that you
have the power
to give life

never forget
to use it

-the power of life and death

you never expect
the moment
when life
breaks through
the cracks
and swallows
you whole

you never expect
the moments
where the sadness
shatters your peace
like a hammer
brought to bear
against a mirror

we can't anticipate
the darkest moments
but we can learn
to live
through them

-expect

never forget
that love
will always
break through

when you
need it
most

-*love will be there*

your mistakes
may hang over you
like a rain cloud

your pain
may haunt you
on and on

but that
is not
who you are

you are
the light
that bursts through
the clouds

you are
the dawning
of the new day

so pick yourself up
go, live your life
and be
what you know
you can be

-*what you are*

forgive
as you
have been
forgiven

-forgivness

love others
even
when they don't
deserve it

-love

you might be
lost
and broken
right now
but you
will not
stay
that way

trust me
things
will
get
better

-*things will get better*

brokenness
is not
a label
that will follow you
for the rest of
your life

brokenness
is merely a bridge
between where you were
and all the places
you'll go

-brokenness is a journey

thank you for reading
please leave a review on amazon

and read my other books

this
is the second chapter
in a long series

tell your friends
thank you

67198184R00078

Made in the USA
Lexington, KY
04 September 2017